Dedicated to our girls, Nicole & Sara,
with love.

Published by
Dreamdust Studios Press
1124 N. Howard Street, Glendale, CA 91027
www.dreamduststudios.com

Written and Illustrated by
Chris Antoine & Bob Prado
ISBN: 978-0692888179

Daisy Dew Drop™

- in -

"Hide 'n Seek Surprise"

Written and Illustrated by

Chris Antoine & Bob Prado

Daisy Dew Drop is a girl

who lives inside a special world.

The Rainbow Garden is a place

that brings a smile to every face.

Where nature is a work of art

helped by Daisy's magic heart.

One morning she went out to meet

her best friend, so small and sweet.

She said, "Fuzzie, let's go play

on this sunny summer day."

Their favorite game
was Hide 'n Seek,
and Fuzzie knew
she wouldn't peek.

So Fuzzie was
the first to hide,
and Daisy covered
up her eyes.

While Daisy counted,

"One. Two. Three..."

Fuzzie thought,

"She won't find me."

"Behind a twig?

Oooops!

Too big."

"Under a rock?

Not a good spot."

"Where's a good place

I can hide?"

the little caterpillar sighed.

Searching in a nearby thicket

she asked Joe the Country Cricket,

"Might you know where Fuzzie's at?"

He just shrugged and tipped his hat.

She asked the ladies having tea,

"Where could little Fuzzie be?"

They looked at Daisy and they said,

"Have you checked the flower bed?"

As Daisy wandered down the trail,

she came upon the Slowpoke Snails.

So Daisy asked them, "Have you seen...

...my fuzzy friend who's pink and green?"

Startled by Antoine the Spider,

who suddenly dropped down beside her,

said, "Fuzzie? She went down zee hill,

past zee tulips and zee daffodils."

A surprise was waiting

round the bend,

Daisy's rough

and rowdy friend.

Dandy Lion

roared with glee,

"I just chased Fuzzie

up a tree!"

When Daisy met some busy bees

and politely asked them, "Please...

have you seen my friend so small?"

"No," they buzzed. "Not at all."

Daisy had searched all day long,

but everywhere she looked was wrong.

Up.

And

down.

And all around.

But Fuzzie just could not be found.

Then suddenly she spied a face,

wrapped inside a veil of lace.

Daisy pondered what to do

to free her friend from this cocoon.

"A sprinkle of enchanted dust,

might do the trick."

she said. "It must!"

Daisy tossed some

from her locket.

Then turned away.

She could not watch it.

Then something floated past her eye.

A pretty yellow butterfly.

"I think I've seen your face before,

on someone else that I adore."

"Remember when you were so round,
and only crawled upon the ground?
Oh, Fuzzie," she could only sputter,
"a better name for you is Flutter!"

About the Authors

Bob Prado and Chris Antoine are long-time creative partners who met while working at the Walt Disney Company. Bob's career has spanned decades drawing some of the planet's best known characters, while Chris has created a library of graphic design programs for animated film and television properties. They combined their talents and formed Dreamdust Studios to fulfill their dreams of creating family friendly properties for the young and young-at-heart. They reside with their families in sunny Southern California.

Learn more about Chris & Bob at: www.dreamduststudios.com
Contacts: chris@dreamduststudios.com, and bob@dreamduststudios.com
See more about Daisy and her friends at: www.daisydewdrop.com
See Daisy's video at: www.youtube.com/watch?v=AHAtiRq_czM
Facebook: https://www.facebook.com/search/top/?q=daisy%20dew%20drop

Daisy
Dew Drop
and the
Rainbow Garden™

Look for Daisy and all her Rainbow Garden friends
in more books and other products coming soon!

www.ingramcontent.com/pod-product-compliance
Lightning Source LLC
Chambersburg PA
CBHW041222040426
42443CB00002B/49

9780692888179